Pentecostalism in Africa

Pentecostalism in Africa
Experiences from Ghana's Charismatic Ministries

J. Kwabena Asamoah-Gyadu

Copyright © J. Kwabena Asamoah-Gyadu 2020

First published 2020 by Regnum Books International

This book is an abridged version of J. Kwabena Asamoah-Gyadu's *Contemporary Pentecostal Christianity* (Oxford: Regnum, 2013), with thanks to David Cranston for his editorial work.

Regnum is an imprint of the Oxford Centre for Mission Studies
St. Philip and St. James Church
Woodstock Road, Oxford OX2 6HR, UK
www.ocms.ac.uk/regnum

The right of Paul Woods to be identified as the Author of this Work has been asserted by him in accordance with the Copyright, Designs and Patents Act 1988.

All rights reserved. No part of this publication may be reproduced, stored in a retrieval system, or transmitted in any form or by any means, electric, mechanical, photocopying, recording or otherwise, without the prior permission of the publisher or a licence permitting restricted copying. In the UK such licences are issued by the Copyright Licensing Agency, 90 Tottenham Court Road, London W1P 9HE.

British Library Cataloguing in Publication Data. A catalogue record for this book is available from the British Library.

ISBN: 978-1-5064-8373-3
eBook ISBN: 978-1-5064-8395-5

Typeset in Candara by Words by Design.

Photo by hao wang on Unsplash

The publication of this volume is made possible through the financial assistance of Evangelisches Missionswerk.

Distributed by Fortress Press in the US, Canada, India, and Brazil

Contents

Foreword	vii
Clothed with Power: Spirit-Inspired Renewal and Christianity in Africa	1
Signs of the Spirit: Worship as Experience	9
Jericho Hour: Prayer as Theological Interventionist Strategy	17
The 12/70 Paradigm Shift: Ecclesiology in the New Charismatic Ministries	25
'For Open Doors': Interpretations of Giving Tithes and Types of Offerings	31
Calvary to Pentecost: The Cross and Prosperity	41
Unction to Function: The Reinvention of the Theology of Anointing	49
Miracle Meal: The Holy Communion – Encountering the Power of the Spirit at the Meal	57
Bible-Believing and Bible-Preaching Churches	61
Conclusion: 'The Spirit Moveth'	67

Foreword by Allan Anderson

Kwabena Asamoah-Gyadu has emerged as the foremost African scholar of Pentecostalism in Africa since the premature passing away of Ogbu Kalu in January 2009. His writings are prodigious and insightful, and the publication of this welcome new book is no exception. I think it is his best study to date, written with the maturity of a scholar who not only observes but also reflects. He writes with the heart of a Christian teacher for truth. It is all too easy for westerners to observe African Pentecostalism from a distance and be critical of their sometimes-bizarre manifestations and emphases on health and wealth in the midst of a poverty-ravished continent. But Asamoah-Gyadu tells it like it is and from the inside, being both a critical and a sympathetic observer. This is a theology of African Pentecostalism, as well as a rich description of its inner heart. Based on extensive research in Ghana and elsewhere, with many vivid descriptions of Pentecostal practices observed by the author, interspersed with theological and biblical reflection, and interacting with other scholars worldwide, this book is essential reading for anyone wanting to understand the rapidly growing and increasingly dominant form of Christianity in the vast African continent. African

Pentecostals will recognise themselves in these pages. This is no caricature of their beliefs and practices, but rather it is a faithful reflection of them. Kwabena Asamoah-Gyadu portrays the critical theological features of African Pentecostalism brilliantly, and I warmly commend this study to you.

Clothed with Power: Spirit-Inspired Renewal and Christianity in Africa

Pentecostalism has emerged as the most exciting and dominant stream of Christianity in the twenty-first century. This is especially so in the non-Western world – Africa, Asia, and Latin America – which is now the heartland of world Christianity. Even in contexts where Christianity may be declining, such as the northern continents, Pentecostalism and its historically younger and theologically more versatile progenies are leading the way in the revival of a Christian presence, which includes the ministries of immigrant churches. The rise of contemporary Pentecostalism and the revival of Christianity give practical expression to the work of the Spirit as blowing wind, a description used metaphorically by Jesus Christ in his encounter with Nicodemus in John 3.

This book examines the importance of pneumatic movements to the renewal of Christianity within the African context. Pentecostalism, the most globalised form of pneumatic Christianity, belongs to the larger Protestant family, and it shares the traditional evangelical theological emphases on the authority of the Bible, the centrality of the cross, regeneration as the way to Christian salvation, and a call to holiness as the outflow of a new relationship with Christ. In addition to these theological themes, Pentecostal and charismatic movements became the 'third force' of Christendom – following Roman Catholicism and mainline Protestantism – at the beginning of the twentieth century. The unique contribution of Pentecostalism to world Christianity lies in the emphasis placed on the experience and power of the Holy Spirit. Pentecostalism developed because many of the historic mainline Protestantism took an intellectual and liberal attitude to the Scriptures and, in the process, neglected the experiential elements of Christianity.

Pentecost and the Renewal of World Christianity

Pentecostalism is a revivalist movement that likes to be biblical in orientation, inspired particularly by developments in the Acts of the Apostles. Its biblical appeal in contemporary Christianity is inspired in part by Peter's response to the crowd that heard him preach on the day of Pentecost. When Peter had preached so powerfully on what God has accomplished in Jesus Christ, the people asked the apostles, 'Brothers, what shall we do?' Peter responded, 'Repent and be baptised, every one of you, in the name of Jesus Christ for the forgiveness of your sins. And you will receive the gift of the Holy Spirit. The promise is for you and your children and for all who are far off – for all whom the Lord our God will call' (Acts 2:38-39). Pentecostals take this promise seriously, especially looking forward to the fact that it could be fulfilled in the life of the church in our times. Until the middle of the twentieth century, Pentecostalism remained a religion on the margins of world Christianity. Today it is impossible to talk about world Christianity without reference to Pentecostalism. In 2008 the John Templeton Foundation, through the University of Southern California, for example, made available US $3.5 million for research on Pentecostalism worldwide, which was an indication of how important this stream of Christianity had become.

Pentecost and the Charismatic Experience

Contemporary manifestations of Pentecostalism are often classified in terms of 'charismatic renewal' as a result of their orientation towards the restoration of the gifts of the Spirit, which include speaking in tongues, prophecy, healing, visions, and revelations. One of the key texts inspiring charismatic renewal worldwide is the vision of dry bones encountered in Ezekiel 37. In most popular Pentecostal interpretations of that passage, the 'valley of dry bones' refers to moribund Christianity or dead churches paralyzed by neglect of the fundamental biblical truths of regeneration by water and the Spirit, by moral permissiveness, and by relativism that reduces the Bible into mere text rather than an active and living truth of divine inspiration.

The expression 'charismatic' comes from *charismata*, meaning 'gifts of grace'. 'Charismatic' is used to refer to renewal prayer fellowships and analogous movements operating within and without historic mission denominations, with the aim of revitalizing the church and Christian life through the restoration of the *charismata pneumatika*, the spiritual gifts. The spiritual gifts, according to Paul, are offered to all (I Corinthians 12:7), and for Pentecostals, shared experiences of the Spirit bring them together as participants to function in their graces for ministry. Pneumatic revivals take place both inside and outside existing churches and denominations believing that that signs and wonders should accompany the ministry of today's church as they did in the ministry of the apostles in Acts. These pneumatic Christian reforms have been part of African Christianity since the beginning of the twentieth century. Pentecostalism, in both its older classical and newer charismatic forms, has now taken over as the representative face of Christianity in Africa.

Charismatic Renewal and the Church Today

The restoration of *charismata pneumatika*, gifts of the Spirit, as part of normal church life can be understood theologically as the reactivation in Christian communities of capacities that have long remained dormant in the life of the church. Whether we refer to them as renewal, restoration, or revival movements, the single most important characteristic of contemporary charismatic movements is the experience of the Holy Spirit. Many churches now open us to charismatic renewal and most of the African immigrant churches emerging in Europe have a charismatic culture.

Many of the Pentecostal churches have developed mega-size congregations that are led by charismatic personalities who preach motivational messages and take very contemporary and modern media-driven approaches to worship. Contemporary Pentecostal churches appeal greatly to upwardly mobile young Christians who are disenchanted with the denominationalism and clericalism of the past. The neo-Pentecostal family also includes trans-denominational Pentecostal fellowships like the Full Gospel Businessmen's Fellowship International and Women Aglow movements, which are lay charismatic parachurch organisations that encourage 'responsible church membership'. This is a policy that helps to facilitate renewal within non-Pentecostal historic mission denominations.

The rise of neo-Pentecostalism was the result of disenchantment with existing religious traditions, the erosion of denominational loyalties and the liturgical conservatism that young people in particular found within historic mission Christianity. The essential nature of neo-Pentecostalism is trans-denominational because the experience of the Holy Spirit is understood to transcend denominational walls, while it clarifies and underscores what is authentically Christian in each tradition without demanding structural or even doctrinal changes in any given church body.

Historic Mission Churches and the Challenge of Renewal

The rise of independent indigenous Pentecostal church movements in Africa through the disenchantment with the historic mission denominations can be illustrated with the rise of the Musama Disco Christo Church (MDCC) in Ghana. The MDCC is one of the biggest and oldest African churches in Ghana. Its name means 'Church of the Army of the Cross of Christ'. In 1923, when a Ghanaian Methodist catechist William Egyanka Appiah started speaking in tongues, seeing visions, prophesying, and healing the sick through prayer, he and his sympathisers were told by the Methodist Church authorities to stop what were described as their 'occult' activities. This attitude towards Holy Spirit phenomena cost the historic mission denominations dearly, in terms of membership, and by the close of the twentieth century their stance had softened in many ways. Almost a century later, most historic mission churches have started to accommodate charismatic renewal groups and phenomena within their ranks to facilitate their survival.

Until this change in attitude, many members of historic mission denominations, while maintaining their allegiance to the mother churches on Sundays, would go in search of relevant Christian experiences elsewhere in one or other of the independent churches during the week. In the mid 1960s, the Presbyterian Church of Ghana Synod, for example, expressed concern that large numbers of people left the denomination to join a Spiritual church, as the independent churches are called, or to attend meetings of healers and prophets. In the process, the Presbyterian Church claimed, they adopted practices unfamiliar to Presbyterian Church life, such as speaking in tongues, organisation of sessions on healing and deliverance, and all-night vigils characterised by loud extemporaneous prayers, prophecies, visions, and revelations. One of the conclusions of the Synod was that a large number of Christians joined them because they were disappointed with their regular churches, in this case the Presbyterian Church, where the worship was considered to be dull with no spiritual power and little prayer.

Eventually, a committee set up by the Presbyterian Church to advise the denomination on how to deal with membership decline and disenchantment suggested that the older churches should recognise the emerging charismatic renewal groups within the denomination to curb the loss of members. This is how from the 1970s, Ghanaian historic mission denominations learnt to have a more tolerant response to charismatic renewal as an authentic biblical and Christian experience.

Conclusion: Spirit Renewal and Ministry

We have talked about the fact that the Pentecostal movement is founded on the biblical truth that the presence of the Holy Spirit could be experienced by people today based on the promise of Jesus. In John 14:18, Jesus had promised his disciples that he was not going to leave them orphaned and that he was going to return. This meant the withdrawal of Jesus' physical presence was not going to mark the end of his presence in the world. He fulfilled his promise to return to the disciples in the power of the Holy Spirit as Comforter and Counsellor. The whole religious philosophy of Pentecostalism is that the promise of the outpouring of the Holy Spirit, that was fulfilled on the day of Pentecost, is something that can be experienced in the life of the church today.

Although there are many criticisms that are levelled against the Pentecostal movement, I take a very positive view of pneumatic Christianity. The impressive congregations they have built, the attractiveness to our upwardly mobile young people, the kinds of media ministries they have developed, and the religious menu they constantly roll out for the public tells me that unless the older churches raise their game, their future will not be that bright. Africa has learnt much from European theology, but Europe in turn may need to learn a few things from the types of immigrant charismatic communities working in their midst. The Protestant churches could in grateful joy, see the work of the Holy Spirit outside the confines of their own organised pastoral activities, recognising the genesis of new churches and congregations on European soil as the grace of God.

Signs of the Spirit: Worship as Experience

One the unique features of Pentecostalism or pneumatic Christianity, is the very expressive, expectant, dynamic, exuberant, experiential, and interventionist nature of its worship. It is through the blessings of its experiential worship that Pentecostalism has had its most significant influence on world Christianity. The experiences that characterise Pentecostal worship include speaking in tongues, revelations, prophecies, healing, exorcism or deliverance, and other pneumatic phenomena that are interpreted as the descent of the Spirit upon worshippers.

Although Pentecostalism is a global movement, there are specific ways in which African Christians have appropriated its spirituality to serve their local needs. For example, when Ghanaian Christians leave older historic mission churches for Pentecostal churches, they do so partly because they find new forms of worship that are not just biblically rooted, but also resonate with indigenous religious traditions. In African traditional worship there is greater freedom of movement, spontaneity, and gaiety than one finds in most older Christian churches, where the atmosphere is often formal and where pews, altars, and pulpits restrict movement.

Understanding Worship

Worship is the highest form of religious expression, and it consists of offering homage and adoration to God. In the Old Testament, we encounter the fact that Yahweh must be worshipped not only because he is the creator God but also because he is the source of the salvation and liberation of his people (cf. Ps. 103). Worship is the celebration of the acts of God in history and ultimately the revelation of himself in Jesus Christ.

When Pentecostal/charismatic Christians meet together in worship, it is to celebrate the power of Jesus in human life as Saviour, as Baptiser in the Holy Spirit, as Healer, and the King who is to return to earth. It is in the context of corporate worship that the gifts of the Spirit that this Jesus has poured out on his church is fully displayed. As Paul says, 'Let the message of Christ dwell among you richly as you teach and admonish one another with all wisdom through psalms, hymns, and songs from the Spirit, singing to God with gratitude in your hearts' (Col. 3:16). Worship, as a continuous experience in the anointing of the Holy Spirit is the heartbeat of Pentecostal Christianity.

Worship in Pentecostal Experience

Pentecostals trace the roots of the worldwide movement to a 1906 revival that broke out at Azusa Street under the leadership of a black preacher, William J. Seymour. The following description of how corporate worship took place in the historical context of the Azusa Street Mission, in Los Angeles between 1906 and 1915, has become a model for contemporary forms of Pentecostal worship:

The intensity of their encounter with God led many at the mission to respond in ways that before their encounter they could 'only imagine.' It was a life-changing moment, a transformative time that produced a range of responses. There were those who, 'surrounded by His glory' at the mission, broke into dance. Others jumped, or stood with hands outstretched, or sang or shouted with all the gusto they could muster. Others were so full of awe when they encountered God that their knees buckled – they fell to the floor, 'slain in the Spirit.' Some spoke, rapid-fire, in a tongue they did not know, while others were struck entirely speechless.

This sort of exuberant form of worship plays out in Pentecostal churches all the time. In Ghana during a visit one Sunday to the Living Streams Ministries International, this charismatic church was concluding a 21-day prayer and fasting programme. The service started with spontaneous mass prayers. Many, including the leader of the session, prayed loudly in tongues. The service then moved into the segment referred to in Pentecostal discourses as praise and worship. This element of the worship involved the singing of choruses accompanied by high amperage keyboard music with jazz instruments, hand clapping, and vigorous youthful dancing, or 'hallelujah-dancing' as it is called. When the worship hit fever pitch, the tempo of the music was reduced. With appropriate gestures – hand raising, prostration, kneeling, weeping, and other symbolic and emotional expressions – people literally abandoned themselves in worship before God. The songs, a blend of locally composed and internationally known gospel-life tunes, affirmed God as holy, awesome, powerful, and majestic. The praise and worship session concluded with further extempore mass prayers, which were summarised by the leader.

If this experience had occurred during non-Pentecostal worship, it would have appeared to be a disorderly or disruptive conduct in church. For these Pentecostals, however, the commotion was a sign of something more profound – divine visitation in worship.

Pentecostal Worship and Primal Spirituality

In Pentecostal spirituality, worship is expected to be participatory, and it must aim at edifying the saints, especially in the use of pneumatic phenomena. Music and pneumatic manifestations of Pentecostal worship are understood to stand in historic continuity with the experiences of the early church as recorded in the Acts of the Apostles and the Pauline epistles. In these biblical narratives, worship seems to have consisted of the singing of hymns, ministry of the word, relating of divine revelations, speaking in tongues, interpretation of tongues, revealing of words of knowledge, and prophesying (1 Cor. 14:26-39).

For Pentecostals, the Holy Spirit not only possesses people during corporate worship but also saturates the atmosphere with his presence. We have noted that this form of pneumatic Christianity resonates much with African religious cultures, also referred to as primal spirituality. Spirit possession is critical in this endeavour, for during other African festival celebrations, possession by spirits constitutes the highest point for participants. The important ingredients of Pentecostal worship – praise, adoration, blessing, and thanksgiving of God in spontaneous singing and voluble prayer in words and tongues accompanied by appropriate gestures, therefore easily strike responsive cords in the African religious imagination.

Pentecostalism is the most experiential branch of Christianity and comes across as a protest movement against dry denominationalism. While the beliefs of historic mission churches may be embodied in codified creeds, formal theological systems, icons, and ordered liturgical structures, those of Pentecostalism are usually embedded in testimonies, ecstatic speech, and bodily movement.

Glossolalia in Worship

Glossolalia, or speaking in tongues, is one of the core-defining characteristics of Pentecostalism. This is the Spirit-inspired utterance that Pentecostals believe must accompany the baptism in the Holy Spirit following conversion. Tongues constitute unintelligible speech that is directed toward God (1 Cor. 14:2, 14-15, 28), and although Paul does not forbid the use of tongues in the assembly, he does not encourage its use as a form of public prayer. What Paul makes clear, is that spontaneous prophecy could be delivered in tongues and interpreted in the context of corporate worship. Paul held tongues speaking in the highest esteem, as a means of communing with God. To that end, his reference to 'inarticulate groaning too deep for words' in Romans 8:26-27 must be understood as referring primarily to glossolalia.

Some of my own most profound moments in Pentecostal worship have occurred when people who possess that grace have sung in tongues. This can lift both the singer and the listeners to another level of spiritual experience. It is an overwhelming and edifying experience that makes the presence of God palpable when it occurs during worship. Tom Smail in his book *In Spirit and in Truth: Reflections on Charismatic Worship* describes the phenomenon of singing in the Spirit as a form of collective religious experience. I am not oblivious to the fact that in the assembly of the church or of God's people, rational prayer is expected to take precedence over irrational utterances. However, speaking in tongues, or glossolalia, still has a place in worship. It enables individuals so empowered with that grace to speak mysteries unto God.

Charismata Pneumatika in Worship

Closely related to the significance of tongues in Christian worship is the use of what Paul describes as *charismata pneumatika*, graces of the Spirit. The expression 'charismata' comes from Paul's writings, and he puts the emphasis on the divine character of the gifts. Thus in 1 Corinthians 14:1-12, he highlights the place of prophecy in Christian worship. Unlike speaking in tongues, which is essentially communion of an individual with God, the prophetic ministry is one that builds up, and exhorts, and comforts.

The worship activities described by Paul had both vertical and horizontal implications, because they were directed towards God on the one hand and towards the community on the other. Participation in worship is a participation in ministry because the essence of ministry is to be open to the Holy Spirit. When worship as ministry touches others, they are always edified and the purpose of gathering as God's people is also fulfilled.

In traditional religion, as in Pentecostalism today, drums, music and dance work together to invoke the presence of the supernatural realm into the natural. Thus drumming, dancing, 'speaking in strange tongues', prophesying, and other such manifestations of exuberance in worship are all critical features that are as much a part of Pentecostalism as they have always been of traditional African religious festivals.

Worship as Encountering God

Paul Tillich indicted Protestantism for replacing ecstatic experiences in religion with doctrinal and moral structures. One of the biggest problems that African Pentecostals have had with historic mission Christianity is the frequent paucity of the latter's worship, especially when it is done because of ritualistic tradition.

African religions pay a great deal of attention to the search for divine intervention in a precarious environment of perilous spirits and witches. In that respect, Pentecostalism has proven popular in Africa because by integrating spiritual practices such as healing and exorcism into worship through ministration, it provides ritual contexts within which people may experience God's presence and power in forceful and demonstrable ways.

Music also plays a critical role in this therapeutic and edifying process of Pentecostal/charismatic worship. Pentecostals worship in expectation that in the midst of the singing and prayer the presence of the Holy Spirit would be felt, and that people will encounter his presence as he does so. It is a mode of religious expression that appeals very much to African religious sensibilities because of its experiential and therapeutic nature. The healing ministries that Pentecostals practice tell us that the issues of health and sickness are not private; they belong to the realm of public liturgy and for those who need help.

Conclusion

In Pentecostal thought, to worship is to respond to the Holy Spirit as God's inspiring, transforming, assuring, healing, and empowering presence. Indeed, as we have seen in this chapter, Pentecostal/charismatic renewal movements and churches constitute a critique to the staid and over-formalised liturgical forms of worship found in many historic mission denominations. In the new type of pneumatic Christianity burgeoning in Africa, God has raised a new breed of churches that are pointing the way to the recovery of worship as the context for encountering a living God who truly inhabits the praise of his people.

Jericho Hour: Prayer as Theological Interventionist Strategy

Jericho Hour, a name taken from Joshua 6, was the original name of a weekly prayer service instituted by Bishop James Saah of the Action Chapel International (ACI), Accra, Ghana, in 1998 (the name has since been changed to 'Dominion Hour' but the principle behind it has not changed). When Jericho Hour began, Saah felt God asking him to establish a 'prophetic prayer service' where 'giant problems would receive giant solutions'. It started with fewer than 30 people, but by 2000 the meeting was attracting the huge numbers we are witnessing today, which is upwards of 3,000 people. Jericho Hour takes place on Thursday mornings and it has done so since its establishment.

In its modern-day re-enactment, the walls of Jericho are those problems – whether physical or spiritual – that prevent people from breaking through in life. At these meetings, participants determine their own postures in prayer, although most people stand throughout the three-hour sessions. Jericho Hour can be extremely noisy. The Prayer Cathedral of ACI usually fills up around 10:00 am with participants mostly on their feet until proceedings end with an offering and blessing around noon. At Jericho Hour the prayers for opportunities to travel occur in the same breath as those asking for marriage, business, health, and employment. The issues prayed about are many and varied, but in my years of observation, it seems to me that the single most important focus is on inveighing against one's enemies, that the power of God might flow into human endeavours.

Prayer and Pentecostal Experiential Spirituality

Studying prayer allows one to understand Pentecostal Christianity through its major strength, and that is, its focus on the experiential aspects of religion. In contrast to the historic mission denominations, Pentecostalism is a movement which emphasises the experience of God and the emotions, whether in prayer, worship, or functioning in the spiritual gifts.

Historically the situation in Africa has not been any different from what took place in the West when charismatic renewal movements emerged to revitalise mainline Christianity. Whereas in evangelical Christianity it became customary to warn people against the expression of feelings and emotions in worship, Pentecostal/ charismatic Christianity chose a different path with its free expressions of noise, tears, smiles, and laughter in God's presence. Prayer is one area in which this difference between Pentecostalism and its older compatriots is evident. In the older liturgical traditions, prayer is read, and so God is approached through the voices of others in written prayers.

The simple repetition of the Lord's Prayer is, for example, never part of any African Pentecostal service because, in Pentecostal thought,

Jesus only taught his disciples the pattern of prayer they were to follow and did not necessarily expect them to repeat it. Pentecostal prayer is expected to be original, long, sustained, and spontaneous, an outflow of the experience of the Holy Spirit.

Prayer and Charismatic Authority

In keeping with Christian theological understanding, Pentecostals pray in the name of Jesus Christ and in the power of the Holy Spirit. The high points of those experiences are when messages of prophecy come through during times of worship. The Holy Spirit is understood as able to lead people in any direction or to become manifest in unpredictable ways. This understanding makes Pentecostals uncomfortable and critical of worship life that appears too ordered. We learn from Pentecostal modes of prayer that the experience of God is not just an emotional one. It is the experience of God acting. The charismatic movement emphasises that God is involved in our world. Its understanding of this involvement is characteristically interventionist because prayer emphasises the irresistible power of God to do things, especially to bring healing

It is against the backdrop of this interventionist theology of prayer that contemporary Pentecostals talk about prayer in terms of a spiritual warfare, and Paul endorses praying in tongues because it is through such prayer that the Spirit helps believers to overcome the weakness evident in the limitations of their language as they seek to communicate with God (Romans 8:26).

Prayer, Warfare and Goliath Hermeneutics

In African Pentecostalism there is often a close relationship between warfare prayer and prosperity. This character of prayer is in keeping with traditional African spirituality, which recognises a transcendent dimension to life that is experienced in the midst of everyday activities. Charismatic testimonies often imply that God does exist and delivers on his word to those who are faithful in their Christianity through the payment of tithes and offerings. Testimonies often include acknowledgement of God as the source not only of wealth, but also of health, employment, promotion, opportunities to travel abroad, secure family life, and personal satisfaction and fulfilment, things that Western society takes for granted.

In contemporary Pentecostalism demons are metaphorically described as Goliaths. Although slain by David several thousands of years ago, Goliath's spirit lives on. 'Goliath has children,' as one person remarked. These modern Goliaths are the demon spirits that work to deny the fulfilment of people's God-given destiny. Goliath is defined as any stubborn problem that keeps threatening, troubling, and tormenting one's life. In African Pentecostal publications on the subject, the five stones that David picked to defeat Goliath represent the letters in the name of J-E-S-U-S, and a whole arsenal of 'Goliath Killing Prayers' has been developed to help overcome those stumbling blocks.

Warfare prayers needed to overcome the Goliaths of life are expected to be aggressive, long, and sustained. This is where all-night prayer vigils and extended daytime prayers like Jericho Hour come in. These are designed, as the new name of the Jericho Hour makes clear, to take dominion over principalities and powers so that human well-being and abundance of life in Christ would be assured.

Praying in the Spirit

Pentecostals teach that all Christians may, and indeed should, experience a baptism of the Holy Spirit after being born-again. This doctrine flows from the conviction that the Spirit came upon the disciples at Pentecost and they spoke in tongues. This experience is seen as a model of all Christian experience related to the encounter with the Holy Spirit.

On the specific meaning of tongues as praying in the Spirit, this is understood as prayer from the heart that springs from and awareness of God, of self, of others, of needs, and of Christ. Whether it comes verbalised, as in the prayers and praises recorded in Scripture, or unverbalized, as when the contemplative gazes Godward in love or the charismatic slips into glossolalia, is immaterial. The idea is that those whose hearts seek God through Christ pray in the Spirit.

In my thinking what distinguishes prayer as a Pentecostal spiritual activity from the understanding of prayer in other Christian traditions is the Pentecostal insistence that praying in the Spirit is distinguished from ordinary prayers by praying in tongues. Christians baptised in the Spirit, according to classical Pentecostal teaching, must speak in tongues and the experience must be sustained in one's prayer life. The Spirit intervenes by interceding for the person praying with what Paul refers to as 'groans too deep for words' (Rom. 8:26).

In addition to comprehending speaking in tongues as a sign of Spirit baptism, contemporary Pentecostals also have a particular understanding of the circumstances within which tongues must be used. Preachers regularly use it to break into their sermons in order to enhance the impression that what they preach is Spirit-inspired or even God-breathed. Tongues are also used as means of spiritual warfare.

Tongues may be abused by some, but there is no need to be so dismissive of the subjective religious experiences and expressions of others. I too have observed the so-called quasi-magical uses of tongues in Ghana, but there is no reason to believe that they necessarily amount to wrongful uses of the gift. The use of tongues, in addition to prayer and prophecy, is considered a very potent form of prayer during crisis. Consider for example the near-tragic experience of Apostle Michael Ntumy, a former chairman of Ghana's Church of Pentecost. Apostle Ntumy was viciously attacked by a machete-wielding assailant one evening in front of his official residence in Accra. 'As the man raised the machete to strike me,' he later explained, 'I fell into a drain by the roadside. I started speaking 'our tongues' and as soon as I burst out into tongues, the man jumped onto his motorbike and fled.' He added, 'the tongues saved my life.'

Strategies of Prayer

In Pentecostal spirituality, very distinct strategies are often thought to make certain prayers more effective than others. The fundamental requirement is faith, but additionally, prayers are considered more effective if they are based on Scripture, said in tongues, proclaimed with authority, militant, use words that resist the devil, and ask for the fulfilment of specific promises.

Prayer strategies have developed with the establishment of prayer places of different sizes and appearance where people can assemble to pray. These prayer places are part of a strategy to translate the dominance of spiritual spaces into the physical realm and to get people to articulate their deep-seated needs and concerns before God in ways that suit Pentecostal understandings of prayer.

These spaces on mountains and forests help those who pray, especially those who shout and move around, to do so without inconveniencing the public. The core reasons for choosing these locations as places of prayer are, however, religious in nature. These sites are considered places of supernatural revelation and encounter. Their names are very revealing: Shiloh, Canaan, Bethel, Jericho, Sinai, Gethsemane, etc.

Theology of Prayer

In the Pentecostal mindset, prayer, authority, and power go together. Charismatics understand that there is an emotional side to human life and their provision for exuberance of sight, sound, and movement in corporate worship caters to it. Granted, charismatic forms of emotional expression can easily become an exhibitionist routine, but then cool bodily stillness, with solemn fixity of face, can equally easily be the expression of a rigid, heartless formalism by Scriptural standards. There is no doubt that a disorderly liveliness, the overflow of love and joy in God, is preferable to a tidy deadness that lacks both.

Pentecostals sustain the belief in the relationship between prayer and manifestations of the power of God. In Acts 4 we are told that after the disciples had prayed, 'the place where they were assembled together was shaken; and they were all filled with the Holy Spirit, and they spoke the word of God with boldness', and that is what modern day Pentecostals attempt to re-enact in their prayer culture through sessions such as we encounter at the Jericho or Dominion Hour.

The 12/70 Paradigm Shift: Ecclesiology in the New Charismatic Ministries

One of the major aims of the contemporary Pentecostal movement has been to reintroduce into church life what has been described as a 'dynamic charismatic spirituality'. In Christian terms the expression 'charismatic' means extraordinary abilities or graces traceable to the workings of the Spirit. It comes from *charis* and refers to embodiments of grace. *Charismata pneumatika*, graces of the Spirit, in the Pauline context relates to those gifts of the Holy Spirit that are a sign of the presence of God among his people. When believers are allowed the space to use their graces of the Spirit in ministry, the church becomes a living entity in which ministry belongs to all and not just to a theologically trained clerical order.

Tradition, Spirit and Ecclesiology

For the older mission denominations, the ecclesial independence that comes with the experiences of the Spirit has been hard to take, and this accounts for some of the pejorative terms and expressions that the older African independent churches attracted in the early years of the twentieth century. The lack of recognition of the gifts of others stands as the single most important reason for the establishment of indigenous Pentecostal ministries in Christian Africa. Historic mission denominations, on account of their doctrinal pedigree, historical connections to Christian Europe, and finely defined liturgical traditions, tended to limit understandings of ministry to ordination. Ministry in many of these older churches has been monolithic with a clear distinction between the lay and ordained members of the church.

Pentecostalism acknowledges clerical roles too, but on the whole, it remains a lay-oriented movement. Often the preferred designation is 'pastor', which places the emphasis on functionality rather than on position, and the movement has demonstrated an extraordinary ability to get the rank-and-file church members involved in ministry. The Pentecostals argue that Paul envisages the local church as the body of Christ, as a charismatic community, where each member, by definition, has a function within the body, that is a role within the community of faith. This is what defines Pentecostal/charismatic ecclesiology.

There are important ways in which the experience of the Holy Spirit is redefining ecclesiology through contemporary African Pentecostalism. One of the most respected and articulate leaders of the movement is Pastor Joseph Anaba, the founding pastor of the Fountain Gate Chapel International, based in Bolgatanga, Ghana. In addition to his gifts as a revivalist, Anaba has an impressive collection of publications, which contain messages that he has delivered at revival meetings. Two of Anaba's major works are *God's End-Time Militia* and *The 12/70 Paradigm Shift*. *God's End-Time Militia* was written within the context of religious, political, and socio-economic changes that occurred in Ghana between the mid-1970s and mid-1980s, as the initial contemporary Pentecostal churches emerged out of the shadows of the evangelical non-denominational fellowships of the period.

In the years from 1978 to 1983 independent Ghana was confronted with one of its harshest economic crises. This chaotic situation was made worse by severe droughts that hit the country, resulting in bush fires, famine, poverty, and squalor. Ghanaians had to queue for basic essential commodities such as milk, sugar, rice, toiletries, and fuel. The moral situation was discouraging.

Prophecies abounded in those days, with the unanimous theme that God was calling the nation to repentance. There was a call to repentance from various Christian leaders and that was the context for the birth of the contemporary Pentecostal movement. When seen in the light of Old Testament salvation history, the call to repentance had a measure of theological credibility.

The Charismatic Churches and Revolutionary Rhetoric

In the religious context, developments in Ghana were reminiscent of those of the early nineteenth century Second Great Awakenings in North America, in which new religious innovators encouraged religious spontaneity and refused to defer to the interpretation of Scripture of learned theologians.

The new charismatics questioned the traditions of the fathers and the dry denominationalism that characterised much of the older ecclesiology. In line with this position, Pastor Anaba suggested that the established churches with their 'good social standing' had become too ceremonial and had lost their power. For that reason,

God had kept his word, Anaba claimed, and poured out his Spirit on ordinary people to work for him in ministry. The implications of these observations for Christian mission was that it raised up a host of lay preachers and leaders of unusual spiritual ability who played a major role in the spectacular spread of Pentecostalism.

Pastor Anaba referred to the new charismatics as 'God's end-time militia'. Those enlisted in God's end-time militia, with their short, non-academic, and less sophisticated training, were supposedly better equipped because they were armed to engage the forces of evil not with cerebral theology but with the Spirit of God. When ministers with seminary training become complacent and lackadaisical, a new breed of ministers without formal education was raised up as a back-up force, Pastor Anaba argued. In the thinking of the new charismatics, the regular army – that is the historic mission church – was bureaucratic and set in its ways, and had lost much of its ability to deliver God's word with power. Consequently, God had now raised up ordinary men and women and had given them spiritual gifts for a more spiritually relevant, challenging, and dynamic ministry.

However, the attitude whereby established Christianity was denounced as irrelevant, is not untypical of Pentecostalism in general, but in their zeal to establish themselves as God's new paradigm for Christianity, charismatics have tended to throw the baby out with the bath water. Many charismatic ministries in Ghana are now realising their error in dismissing theological training and academic work and not only are they now setting up Bible schools to train prospective pastors, but they are also drawing some of the teachers for these Bible schools from among the clergy of historic denominations that they previously considered spiritually dead.

Ultimately the use of the gifts of the Spirit in ministry must bring glory to God, who revealed himself in Jesus Christ. The evidence of the gifts is an indication that Jesus Christ continues to exercise his ministry in the world through the presence of the Spirit after his Ascension. 'I will not leave you as orphans,' Jesus said, 'I will come to you' (John 14:17).

If charisma is not the preserve of a few, it is also not to be restricted to particular sets of clearly defined gifts, for *whatever* word or act mediates grace to the believing community is charisma. In practice, the charismatic ministries create room for the recognition of people who are specially anointed by God to provide leadership, by recognising the regular ministries as listed in Ephesians 4:11-12.

In my view the democratisation of charisma has made the style of ministry within contemporary Pentecostalism a grace-oriented one in which, instead of relying on hierarchies of ministers or on so-called extraordinary gifts of the Spirit, the laity have been mobilised on the basis of their spiritual gifts and talents to minister in the power of the Spirit in leading worship, in personal evangelism, healing, and deliverance, and in other ways. The many Bible schools that have sprung up among contemporary Pentecostals are not exclusively for training for pastoral ministry.

Conclusion

There is much reference in traditional Western Protestant ecclesiology to the priesthood of all believers and to the ministry as belonging to the 'whole people of God'. In spite of this, the ordained clergy in these churches hold a virtual monopoly over things pertaining to ministry. Within the ecclesiology of the charismatic ministries, the basis of ministry becomes a person's encounter with the Spirit and not theological competence or dynastic succession.

The emphasis on experiencing the Spirit and making use of one's gifts in ministry that stands as one of the key factors accounting for the growth of the charismatic ministries may also ensure their survival from this generation to the next.

'For Open Doors': Interpretations of Giving Tithes and Types of Offerings

There are two regular modes of giving or fundraising in contemporary Pentecostalism, the payment of tithes and the collection of regular offerings. Pentecostal giving is usually described in terms of seed-sowing for which harvests may be expected. When seeds are sown, the faithful are taught to expect various forms of harvest, such as money, jobs, promotions, health, or children. The saying 'offering time', to which worshippers respond, 'blessing time', was introduced into African church life through the contemporary Pentecostals who have popularised tithing within Christianity, turning it into a sacramental duty. This means that tithes and offerings are not mere Christian responsibilities, but also means of securing God's graces in the endeavours of life.

Giving: Biblical Foundations of a Christian Responsibility

One key text related to tithing is Malachi 3:8-12, where the nation is accused of robbing God by not tithing and thereby losing God's blessing. In the New Testament at least four passages mention the tithe. One of them, Matthew 23:23, has Jesus chastising the Pharisees for religiously tithing but neglecting the equally important faith matters of justice, mercy, and faithfulness (cf. Luke 11:42). Tithing is also referred to in the Parable of the Pharisee and the Publican in Luke 18, in which the Pharisee, wanting to justify himself before God, mentions among other things that, 'I give a tenth of everything I get' (Luke 18:12). For many believers in tithes, the ultimate New Testament passage on the issue is Hebrews 7:1-10. This refers to the encounter between Abraham and Melchizedek in terms that connect a pre-Mosaic practice with Christians under the new covenant.

Interpretations

The contemporary Pentecostal churches studied here insist on the payment of tithes as a doctrinal practice with the calculation based on gross, not net, income. In some churches, giving consists of cash and other gifts that go to the pastor as a modern-day Levite, which is also sometimes institutionalised into a 'Pastors' Appreciation Day'. A further level of giving occurs as an honorarium for a guest preacher. On occasion, pastors and prophets of various Pentecostal churches have been accused of using this system of love-offering to scratch each other's backs in a process of indirect personal enrichment. The quantum of honorarium given to guest preachers, it is expected, would be reciprocated later 'with interest' when a host pastor visits his guest's church later.

The Importance of Tithing in Pentecostalism

For contemporary Pentecostal congregations in Africa, tithes bring in substantial amounts of money. This income has enabled many of them to stay independent of foreign-mission financial support. Churches also fund their often-grandiose building projects and media ministries from these tithes. With all kinds of economic recessions in the northern continents and the decline of Christianity in those contexts, the decision by independent churches and contemporary Pentecostals in Africa to be financially independent is very admirable. The founder of the International Central Gospel Church, Pastor Mensa Otabil of Ghana, claims that one of the reasons for his calling into ministry was to challenge the church in Africa to be financially self-sufficient.

The insistence on the payment of tithes is so strong that one Ghanaian pastor is said to have claimed during a broadcast of his television programme that non-tithing Christians were worse than armed robbers. Armed robbers steal from human beings, he noted, but non-tithers steal from God. Whatever the status of this anecdotal statement, there is no doubt that funds raised, whether through tithing, offerings, or special fundraising events, enable the new Pentecostal churches to fund their very expensive programmes and projects, which include the establishment of private universities, television and radio ministries, and the very large cathedrals and worship auditoriums that many of them have been able to build.

Many of the pastors also have access to money and have very comfortable lifestyles that include the building of palatial homes and the use of luxurious cars, or even personal jets. It is now fashionable for the average contemporary Pentecostal pastor to travel first or business class and for his children to be born and educated abroad. The United States of America is the destination of choice. It is therefore important to understand how the theology of tithing and offerings is linked directly to the theology of prosperity in contemporary Pentecostalism.

Giving and Prosperity

An important statement by Jesus Christ used to support the theology of transactional giving is Luke 6:38: 'Give, and it will be given to you. A good measure, pressed down, shaken together and running over, will be poured into your lap. For with the measure you use, it will be measured to you.' This text, regardless of context, is preached and applied almost exclusively to fundraising in Pentecostal/charismatic churches.

A number of contemporary Pentecostal preachers also teach that God will dispossess unbelievers of their wealth and give it to those who will employ that wealth for the purposes of Christian evangelisation and mission. It is not uncommon for pastors to teach that it is contrary to God's will for unbelievers to be rich. The understanding is that wealth in the hands of unbelievers promotes Satan's agenda, but God is putting wealth back into the hands of his chosen people. Believers, it is taught, must move in quickly to take possession, because God is rearranging things to favour his people.

Discipleship, Stewardship and Theology of Giving

The teaching on giving has generated within African Pentecostalism an incredibly high sense and spirit of generosity, unparalleled in the history of the church in Africa. That all resources belong to God in the same way that our bodies belong to him as temples of the Holy Spirit is certainly an important theological position. Christian discipleship encapsulates yielding one's life to God in Christ and by the power of the Holy Spirit living a holy life for him. This Christian discipleship is also a call to stewardship, which means Christians must have a holistic sense of giving, which is made possible by first bringing their lives and affairs under the lordship of Jesus Christ.

However, the grace of giving, as discussed by Paul in 2 Corinthians 8, was an outflow of something fundamental that is often missed in the teaching on tithes that identifies a transactional motive for giving. The members of the churches in Macedonia 'gave themselves first to the Lord'. In other words, their giving of money flowed out of a sense of belonging to God and of being part of God's mission by contributing to the resources needed for it.

God may have chosen to bless them in other ways too, but in the context within which they gave, the Macedonians seem to have been moved by the sense that 'belonging to God' was sufficient blessing and therefore provided the primary reason for their giving of their substance towards his work. I believe that even in the midst of extreme poverty and deprivation, there may have been areas of life in which they felt the graces and goodness of God. Judging by the way their state of poverty is described, we cannot look at their circumstances and conclude that they were extremely poor because they had not fulfilled their tithing obligations.

Jesus does indeed call for something more radical than a tenth of our income; he calls for everything, just as he gave himself unconditionally for our salvation. He gave his very life in a generous act of love, not simply to make tithing Christians materially wealthy and non-tithers materially poor, but so that we can be rich towards God. Some of the most faithful Christians in the world, especially in non-Western contexts, also remain some of the poorest people on the planet. What this means is that the theology of transactional giving to God fails to account for the reasons why some faithful tithers do not necessarily see any improvements in their economic circumstances.

Pentecostals do not necessarily speak amiss when they apply the passage in Luke 6:38 to fundraising, whether in tithes or other offerings. However, to consistently interpret this verse exclusively in terms of tithing or giving money is to do serious injustice to the biblical narrative and the issues of social justice that Jesus was trying to raise.

In the new covenant Christians offer a proportion of their wealth as the Lord's rightful due in view of his claim on all that they are and all that he has entrusted to them. When such giving is inspired by the love of Christ, it does not come in calculated percentages that are intended to fulfil old covenantal obligations in new covenantal terms. We give generously and beyond measure in the full knowledge that Christ gave his life for human salvation. Our tithes and offerings thus 'imitate' Jesus' offering, Our money at the altar is not a payment but a symbolic expression of ourselves, which means that giving is part of our worshipful response to God's love in Jesus Christ.

Giving as Worship

Giving is therefore an act of worship. In the Old Testament, the tithing system made provision for worship by ensuring that there was regular financial support of the ministry of the tabernacle and temple (Num. 18:21-23) and by calling on all Israelites to come together for a feast in the presence of the Lord God (Deut. 14:22-23). The tithing system also safeguarded just governance by demanding that support of the sanctuary and its personnel trumped governmental claims to the tithe (cf. 1 Sam. 8:15, 17) and by ensuring adequate compensation for Levites and priests whose call to service precluded their share of landed estates (Num. 18:20-21). Additionally, tithing ensured relief for the poor, foreign residents, orphans, and widows as well as the Levites (Deut. 14:28-29). Tithing therefore formed a response to God for his goodness as well as relationships with others, which enabled the maintenance of both the vertical and horizontal relationships that must characterise meaningful worship.

Christological Hermeneutics in Tithing

On almost every theological issue, it is important that we apply Christological hermeneutics. Interpreting and applying the Bible with the Christ factor in mind. One of the main problems with over-reliance on the Old Testament in the teaching on tithes is that it makes the practice too pharisaic (Luke 11:42-43). In other words, it makes it an outward religious practice devoid of inward affection and reliance on God's grace.

There is nothing wrong with encouraging people to pay tithes as part of Christian duty, but to build this act on a teaching of transactional giving to God is to fail to take account of the workings of the grace of God in human lives and circumstances. In transactional giving, God is treated as a business partner who has to acquiesce to the demands of those who have fulfilled their side of a bargain. Tithing was a religious duty under the old covenant and although there is nothing wrong with making promises to God, the fulfilment of our obligations to God must not be made contingent upon whether or not he acts in our favour.

The transactional approach to giving also challenges the sovereignty of God to determine the destiny of people. Christian giving as seen in the ministry and teaching of Christ must come from the heart and must not be done to win public approval by outward piety.

Christ: God's Indescribable Gift

A further problem in transactional giving is that those who tithe and yet go through pain and disappointment are left confused. The theology of the cross is missing from contemporary Pentecostal understanding of giving. The way tithing is taught takes us back to pre-Reformation days, when people literally paid for the grace of God through the purchase of indulgences. Paul concludes his teaching on giving by describing Jesus Christ as God's 'indescribable gift'. We give to God not to buy his grace, favour, or some heavenly harvest reserved for tithers, but because giving is part of worship and we live in expectation of God's grace.

The general tenor of the teaching of the New Testament is that we give to God faithfully and trust him for his grace in life, knowing that if we sow sparingly, we reap sparingly and if we sow bountifully, we reap bountifully. But that is not a magical formula, because God's hand cannot be twisted in our favour; to think otherwise is to challenge God's sovereignty. The promises of God come true by his grace and we can only trust him to fulfil these promises through his own indescribable gift, Jesus Christ who is Lord and Saviour.

Conclusion

Contemporary Pentecostalism has achieved a lot within African Christianity, but one of the greatest challenges in its approach to Scripture and life is its inability to articulate a proper response to misfortune and deprivation. Life has its joys and its pains. Unfortunately, however, the pains are mostly shelved by the leadership. Ordinary members who are faithful with their tithes have not been helped to come to terms with the fact that although everybody may expect that God will let things go well, sometimes life can take painful courses. Gifford notes how the relentless stress on victory by contemporary Pentecostals in Ghana means that negative realities can only be rejected. When things are not going too well, we do not have to retrieve our tithes in anger and disappointment with God; God must be trusted for his grace to turn the most difficult of circumstances around in our favour.

Calvary to Pentecost: The Cross and Prosperity

John Stott, whose book *The Cross of Christ* has proven to be one of the most influential books on the cross in the last century, points to the Last Supper as a memorial instituted by Jesus to dramatize neither his birth nor his life, neither his words nor his works, but only his death. Stott draws from this that it was above all by his death that Jesus wished to be remembered. He concludes by considering the centrality of the cross in Christianity – it is safe to say, there is no Christianity without the cross. This means if the cross is not central to our religion, ours is not the religion of Jesus. Stott concludes one of the most important chapters of the book by submitting that the cross reinforces three truths – about ourselves, about God and about Jesus Christ. Firstly, he explains, nothing reveals the gravity of human sin like the cross; secondly, the cross reveals that God's love must be wonderful beyond human comprehension; and thirdly, the cross shows that the salvation of Christ must be a free gift.

Catholic theologian Hans Urs von Balthasar also reiterates the profound truth that, 'if theology is to be Christian, then it can only be a theology which understands in dynamic fashion the unsurpassable scandal of the cross.' These are not truths with which any evangelical mind would disagree with and yet within contemporary Pentecostal theological discourses, direct engagement with the truth of the cross often tends to be one-sided by seeking its material blessings and disregarding its shame, something that Jesus never did (Heb. 12:1-2).

Tom Smail, a leader in the European charismatic fraternity, once said, 'The way to Pentecost is Calvary; the Spirit comes from the cross.' Smail explains that he uttered this statement in prophetic tongues at a public meeting of charismatic leaders. When it was interpreted by another participant, the statement, he notes, confirmed things that had been at the centre of his thinking. This episode followed an earlier personal process of renewal that had led to an experience of Holy Spirit baptism. Smail points out that most Christians would agree that there is a relationship between the Spirit and the cross. This connection between Pentecost, representing the outpouring of the Spirit, and the Passion, representing the death of Christ on the cross, has good biblical foundations. In Peter's Pentecost sermon, for example, he declares:

> *Jesus of Nazareth was a man accredited by God to you by miracles, wonders and signs, which God did among you through him, as you yourselves know. This man was handed over to you by God's set purpose and foreknowledge; and you, with the help of wicked men, put him to death by nailing him to the cross ... Therefore let all Israel be assured of this: God has made this Jesus, who you crucified, both Lord and Christ. (Acts 2:22-23, 36)*

When it comes to contemporary Pentecostal theology, however, the emphases of the movement on experience, glory, and power make it difficult for the full meaning of the cross in relation to Pentecost to be sustained.

In talking about the cross in relation to Pentecostalism we will have in mind teachings and practices relating to the message of prosperity as they are understood within contemporary Pentecostalism in Africa. For ardent exponents of the prosperity gospel, any form of misfortune is an indication of the presence of supernatural evil in one form or another. The sort of prosperity gospel that promotes materialism often fails to engage with the hard realities of life and on occasion fails to provide pastoral care for those whose circumstances may not be reflective of its brand of success.

I am not alone in this thinking. In a preliminary but very important article on this subject, Martin Mittelstadt, himself a Pentecostal, discusses the fact that at both the scholarly and ecclesial levels, the Pentecostal tradition has neglected to address and to apply the role of the Holy Spirit in contexts of suffering and persecution. His article provides concrete evidence of how the martyrdom of a Pentecostal missionary in the Congo in 1964 led to the successful planting of a church that has thrived to the present day.

The martyrdom of Stephen is one of the most popular examples of suffering by those who although filled with the Holy Spirit had to suffer humiliation, persecution, and death for the sake of the Gospel (Acts 7).

The Message of the Cross

Jesus referred to the Holy Spirit as the Comforter not just because the Holy Spirit would continue his ministry, but also because he expected his followers to go through times of distress during which they would need a companion in the form of his spiritual presence. As long as we live in this transient and imperfect world, suffering comes to people, sometimes indiscriminately. It may be due to sin, Satan, evil spirits, wrongful choices that we make ourselves or that are made by others on our behalf, or even acts of nature. The God of resurrection and the power of Pentecost must not be dissociated from the God of the cross; he is the same being who also identifies with weakness and shame. It is precisely because Jesus knew that the circumstances of some would be more difficult than the circumstances others, that he made pastoral care an important qualification for entry into the Kingdom of God (Matt. 25:31-46).

Some contemporary Christians, like the Jews and Greeks mentioned by Paul in the first chapter of his first letter to the Corinthians, refuse to come to terms with the fact that God could choose a path of shame and humiliation to serve his purposes. In the early years of contemporary Pentecostalism in Ghana some even refused to celebrate Good Friday, claiming that from the resurrection, God gave a new beginning and that we dishonour God when that which reminds him of the pains of crucifixion is celebrated. The truth of the matter is that the message of the cross was in conflict with the emphases on success, victory, promotion, power, elevation, and breakthrough that were being expounded from the platforms of the new churches. The message of the cross is one that gives thanks to God for victories but puts them in perspective, knowing that calamity, misfortune, pain, poverty, and deprivation can also, at least for the Christian, serve as means of experiencing the glory of God. The experience of Paul provides an important paradigm of what this could mean when he talks about his 'thorn in the flesh':

> *Three times I pleaded with the Lord to take it away from me. But he said to me, 'My grace is sufficient for you, for my strength is made perfect in weakness.' (2 Cor. 12:8-9)*

The Cross in Contemporary Pentecostalism

The triumphalism associated with contemporary Pentecostalism makes it difficult for the movement to appreciate the inseparable relationship between what Smail calls 'the renewing and empowering work of the Spirit' on the one hand and 'the centre of the gospel in the incarnation, death, and resurrection of Jesus Christ' on the other. Contemporary Pentecostal discourse usually dwells around words to do with victory, power, breakthrough and winning, and on other such terms and expressions that deliberately create the impression that the Spirit-filled Christian becomes almost completely insulated from certain misfortunes that afflict other people. This is why at the beginning of the movement in the late 1970s, the words 'worse', 'poorer', and 'sickness' were removed from wedding vows and replaced with 'best', 'richest', and 'prosperity'. In other words, contemporary charismatic theology is very much a theology of glory that deliberately shuts out of fellowship and theological discourse those whose circumstances in life do not reflect sufficiently victory and power.

He Restores My Soul

On one occasion I was called upon without notice to speak some words of exultation at the funeral of a former student of mine who was also a leader of contemporary Pentecostalism in Ghana. The pastor, then 44 years old, had formerly been a member of the Action Chapel International, but had left that church under not so pleasant circumstances to start his own Pneuma Life Church International. In 2010 the pastor had been called home to glory.

The funeral was a public event that was attended by about one thousand mourners and was celebrated in typical contemporary Pentecostal style. The funeral was a celebration of the life of this charismatic pastor and all the messages centred on the fact that our late friend had now disembarked from a plane at the end of his journey. Each speaker called for applause sometime during his or her message and then again at the end of the delivery. I was moved by the celebratory tone of the funeral, but I was also reflecting on the fact that not one of the speakers had paid attention to the plight of a young widow who was mourning the father of her young children.

When I was invited to speak, I told the congregation not to applaud at any time during my presentation. At that point it was not clear to me whether the applause was for the eloquence of the speaker or in appreciation of God for the words they were hearing. I liked the celebration of the pastor's life, but the applause and screams had gone overboard and for me were becoming inappropriate for the occasion. The immediate family members had been traumatised, and it did not appear to me that the pastors cared too much about that. My short message was addressed to the widow and her three children, who were all below twelve years of age. 'Jesus will restore your soul,' I found myself saying, from Psalm 23. I explained that such restoration is needed after a period of bereavement, and the widow was obviously traumatised by the sudden death of a pastor, husband, and father whom she had described in the elaborate funeral brochure as her 'best friend'. It was clear from her tribute that there were hard questions on her mind regarding the sudden death of her husband.

'The only one who can restore your soul in these circumstances,' I noted, is the Lord Jesus Christ who himself knows what trauma looks and feels like. The conclusion to my short address was this: God had called our friend home to glory, but the trauma that this had brought in its wake was not going to be taken away by applause. The widow and her children were going to need the comfort and restoration of the Lord, who knew trauma on the cross. So might the Lord restore the bereaved soul of this widow and all who were deeply affected by this death and who would be left to pick up the pieces when everybody had left the funeral grounds to return to their homes and businesses. The place was quiet, and I knew the point had been made.

Conclusion

Martin Luther and John Stott, were both advocates of a theology of the cross in contemporary Christianity. They drew attention to the fact that when the cross is undermined in Christian preaching and life, faith is emptied of its meaning and power. Luther contrasted what he called *theologia crucis*, 'theology of the cross' with *theologia gloriae*, 'theology of glory', providing a guide for understanding theology through the central symbol of Christianity.

There is no doubting the fact that in the African context, Pentecostalism has contributed to the growth of Christianity and to making Africa one of the major heartlands of global Christianity. Yet in spite of Pentecostalism's massive contribution to the modern reformation and to renewal of the church, the disproportionate neo-Pentecostal emphasis on success and prosperity make it difficult to recognise the close and intimate relationship between the renewing and empowering work of the Spirit and the centre of the gospel in the incarnation, death and resurrection of Jesus. Such a failure creates imbalances for neo-Pentecostal theology because, although we are rejuvenated and empowered at Pentecost, we are judged, corrected and matured at the cross.

Unction to Function:
The Reinvention of the Theology of Anointing

Anointing in contemporary Pentecostalism is usually a metaphor for the presence of the power of God and may enable a person to perform miracles or preach in an effective way drawing many people to Christ. The use of olive oil as a material substance for healing and empowerment is not new in African pneumatic Christianity. It started with the older independent church prophets but has developed as a subculture within African Christianity, with anointing services now taking place in many historic mission churches too.

Anointing is seen as the power of the Holy Spirit in action, as Pastor Eastwood Anaba records:

> *The anointing oil is not synonymous with the Holy Spirit. However, when it is taken from common use and assigned to spiritual purposes it becomes a medium for the transmission of spiritual power. The presence of the Holy Spirit in a place and working of the Holy Spirit in the life of the person carrying the oil, allowing the oil to be used by God as an instrument of power.*

There is a three-fold understanding of anointing in contemporary African Pentecostal thought. First, the most common use of the expression 'anointing' occurs when olive oil is applied to the physically or spiritually sick, accompanied by prayer. The most commonly cited text in support of the practice of anointing the sick with oil comes from James 5:14-15: 'Is any one of you sick? He should call the elders of the church to pray over him and anoint him with oil in the name of the Lord. And the prayer offered in faith will make the sick person well; the Lord will raise him up.' For our present purposes, however, it is important to note from his conclusion that in this text James advocates a continuing ministry of healing that incorporates anointing with oil at the hands of the elders and fervent praying in the expectation that healing will result. Ordinary members, if they are so led by the Spirit, may also anoint the sick with oil. When used as a means of healing, oil may, on occasion, be given to the sick person to drink; in my experience this tends to be the case when the ailments have to do with internal organs.

Second, among African Pentecostals generally the expression 'anointing' is used in close relation to 'charisma'. The former term is frequently employed to describe a person whose ministry is so charismatic that it produces tangible results. This is what one charismatic church pastor meant when he described a person to me as having the 'unction to function'. If a person 'has the anointing' signs, then signs and wonders are believed to accompany his or her ministry, because, as it is often put, 'the anointing brings results'.

Third, the expression 'anointing' is used in the context of special services held in order to mediate to people the presence of God in the power of the Spirit. 'Anointing for Change' and 'Anointing for

Breakthrough' are only two of the various types of anointing that may be available through anointing services. At these anointing services, worshippers can expect to realise success and prosperity in their lives. Through the application of olive oil and prayer, evil is reversed in the lives of people, even of nations and communities, so that they are empowered to deal with the difficulties of life.

Anointing Services

The extensive use of olive oil in African Pentecostalism must be understood, against the backdrop of the desire to effectively mediate God's presence in power, healing, deliverance, and protection against the evils of life.

Typically, anointing services at Winners' Chapel, to use a specific example, begin with praise and worship in song, which is followed by mass extemporaneous prayers, testimonies, and preaching of the word before the service culminates in the anointing with oil. Members are required to bring their own bottles of oil to the service and most purchase some at the premises. The popularity of the anointing services generates a huge market in the sale of olive oil and the white handkerchiefs that are used in the victorious dancing times that conclude the anointing services. The worshippers were invited by their charismatic bishop to pour a little oil into their right palm, place the oiled palm on their forehead, and 'begin to prophesy your freedom'.

People are anointed when they are sick, but they are also anointed when they have needs requiring supernatural intervention. Physical objects may also be anointed, particularly to restrain evil influences upon them, for example, to reverse the presence of evil in haunted homes. The concept of anointing demonstrates very forcefully the strong relationship that exists in African thinking between sin and evil, on the one hand, and sickness and suffering, on the other.

In the case of Pentecostal media preachers, olive oils may even be placed on radios and TV sets during broadcasts, in order to infuse them with power sent through the airwaves for the mediation of health and power.

Advertising the Anointing

Anointing services are usually advertised, and they have become an important avenue through which Pentecostalism spirituality has spread. The use of olive oil at Pentecostal/charismatic meetings has become so widespread that in Ghana, oil is now more often commercially advertised for its religious than its culinary purposes. The extensive use of anointing oil has generated much controversy and debate in the Ghanaian media because of the abuses that have characterised this practice among some Pentecostal/charismatic churches and leaders. In one such case, reported by the magazine *Ghana Review International*, a 24-year-old assistant pastor exposed his senior pastor for commercializing the use of olive oils. The assistant pastor alleged that his boss would send him to buy olive oil on the open market for 15,000 cedis per bottle (approximately $2), which he then resold to members who came for anointing at prices ranging from 500,000 to 2,000,000 cedis (approximately $70–$250).

Concerns occasioned by over-reliance on and unorthodox uses of oil, and indeed of other such instrumentalities of prayer, are genuine, and they must not be taken lightly. The older independent churches of

Africa were very notorious for their dependence on and commercialisation of therapeutic substances, especially 'Florida Water' (a strongly scented perfume), which virtually became a fetish in the hands of church members. Contemporary Pentecostals generally denounce these older independent churches for their over-reliance on African traditional religious strategies of healing, but current indications are that some of these practices have crept into the healing ministries of some modern African Pentecostal churches and leaders.

Anointing and Testimonies

The scepticism amongst the Ghanaian public and in the media that has accompanied the extensive use of olive oil is not unfounded. There are many circumstances in which the use of oil has been controversial, even appearing quasi-magical in the way the oil has been applied and the sorts of things it is claimed the oil is able to do. However, that people are benefiting from anointing as a sacramental procedure for mediating the grace of God is also not in doubt, as testimonies from beneficiaries often declare.

My personal participation in anointing services has brought to my attention many such testimonies from people for whom the application of olive oil has worked. Cripples have walked, barren women have given birth, and various tumours have disappeared as the result of the application of oil following prayer.

In conversations with Ghanaian charismatic Christians regarding how they felt after services where such pneumatic manifestations had occurred, people almost always used the phrase, 'the anointing was great'.

In the anointing theology expressed in the sermons of the new Pentecostals, the healing in Acts 5:15 as Peter's shadow fell on the sick is explained in terms of the anointing upon his life. It is the anointing on Paul that made it possible for handkerchiefs and aprons that had touched his body to heal sicknesses and drive out evil spirits (Acts 29:11). In other words, the anointing accomplishes; it makes things happen.

The anointing oil, therefore, serves as means of empowerment for the fulfilment of one's ambitions by helping the anointed to overcome the obstacles of life. Every New Year's Eve, there are all-night prayer vigils in Ghanaian churches. One of the central rites in Pentecostal/charismatic churches at this time is to anoint worshippers in order that they may gain the needed strength and grace for the ensuing year. That the anointing is done at the dawn of the New Year is very significant. If baptism and the Lord's Supper celebrate the death and resurrection of the Lord Jesus Christ in the life of the Christian and the church, the anointing with oil celebrates the outpouring of the Holy Spirit and the empowerment of the Christian and the church for life and ministry.

Anointing Oil: Symbol of the Holy Spirit

From the biblical perspective, the application of oil as anointing is a sign that draws upon the anointed person the abiding presence of God the Holy Spirit. In the Old Testament, kings, prophets, vessels and other items used in the temple for worship were all anointed with oil in order to consecrate them to the Lord.

The anointing oil that is in wide use among Pentecostal/charismatic Christians today therefore represents the Holy Spirit, who endows people with graces, authority, and power and through that sacrament sets them apart for God's service or ministry. African Pentecostals will often speak of the Spirit's anointing being great upon that person. In many cases, gifts that seemed to have been lying dormant in people have suddenly come back to life, rejuvenating their ministries in powerful and demonstrable ways, after these individuals have been anointed with oil in services of impartation of the Holy Spirit.

Sacrament: Means of Grace

A sacrament is the expression of the divine presence through physical objects. It may well be that the extensive, practical, and innovative ways in which the charismatic churches are using olive oil are directing the church's attention to the sacramental value of oil that has been neglected, particularly in much of modern Protestantism. In the Roman Catholic tradition, oil is used in the consecration of bishops as a symbol of the Holy Spirit. The Catholic sacrament of Extreme Unction also requires the application of olive oil. Augustine explains a sacrament as 'a visible form of an invisible grace'. Exploring the relationship between a sacramental sign and the grace that it signifies, John Calvin emphasised God's deliberate accommodation of human weakness through the sacraments.

Pastor Anaba also comments perceptively from a charismatic Christian perspective as follows:

> *God sometimes chooses to use physical things as means of transmitting his power… We are not to make an idol of the oil, but it must be clear that God in his sovereignty can*

> *impart his power into a physical object for the purpose of ministration.*

The deep theological insights provided by Pastor Anaba on the relationship between the oil and the Spirit constitute the same interpretation that is given the sacramental bread and wine at the Eucharist, that is to say they become a means of grace.

Conclusion: Anointing – Its Power and Dangers

In Ghana, the popularity of the anointing phenomenon seems to have brought pressure on some charismatic pastors to seek the anointing through the application of olive oil in order to enhance their own powers. Anointing is thought to make a leader's ministry extraordinarily effective.

New religious practices have developed around anointing. On occasion people are required to present the symbols of their trade for anointing: travellers bring their passports, office workers bring their pens, seamstresses and tailors bring their scissors, and carpenters bring their tools. The stories of the anointing oil that are recounted make the phenomenon sound quasi-magical.

In one case, it was claimed that the application of anointing oil to the engine of a car that would not start brought the vehicle back to life. The wild stories accompanying anointing testimonies and claims lead Pastor Anaba to rightly caution that great errors arise when we neglect fellowship with the Holy Spirit and the study of God's word. Anointing will become a debilitating problem if it is not practised with integrity and theological soundness.

Miracle Meal: The Holy Communion – Encountering the Power of the Spirit at the Meal

The life of the new community of believers, according to Luke, consisted of four elements: a study of the word, active fellowship, breaking of bread, and prayer (Acts 2:42-47).

In Pentecostal thought, the invocation of the Spirit is at the heart of the meal, and he comes to infuse the elements with his powerful presence intervening in the affairs of life. This understanding as offered by the new Pentecostals involves a close connection between the meal and the theology of prosperity. Both the form and frequency of Holy Communion differs across contemporary Pentecostals groups but in most cases, the Lord's Supper is a source of healing, breakthrough, and general empowerment similar to the sacramental importance of anointing people with oil, bringing transformation and power into the lives and situations of those who have partaken. There is open access at the Lord's Table in contemporary Pentecostal churches as long as people confess Christ as Lord.

Holy Communion in Charismatic Church Settings

In understanding Pentecostal practices in Africa, experience usually moves ahead of reflection, and these churches will usually adapt or pursue religious practices that flow out of belief in what works, rather than take on what might be deemed to be theologically sensible.

Holy Communion and Good Friday as related events are now becoming more central to the activities of Pentecostal churches. In the past, a number of contemporary Pentecostal churches refused to organise worship services on Good Friday on the grounds that the day was associated with pain and suffering. The revised attitude towards Good Friday has translated into how Holy Communion is celebrated. Although Holy Communion has always been celebrated, it appears that there is now much more attention paid to communion and it is celebrated more frequently.

Holy Communion is celebrated to affirm the general orthodox belief that Jesus is the Lamb of God who takes away the sin of the world (John 1:29). However, many Pentecostals in addition, believe in the divine therapeutic value of the communion often testifying to the fact that taking communion has the ability to heal diseases and grant good health and wellbeing. Some believe that members of the early church rarely fell ill because they took Holy Communion regularly.

The only requirement at Winners' Chapel or any other place I visited is that partakers of Holy Communion must have been born-again. At Winners' Chapel in February 2010, the prayer over the elements came after the word and the Altar Call. The prayer was said from a distance, and it simply blessed the elements in the name of Jesus Christ and in the power of the Holy Spirit. The pastor praying declared as part of the blessing of the elements that in partaking of Holy Communion, 'sicknesses will disappear, insomnia will cease, finances will improve; and every expectation of yours will come to pass.'

Conclusion

The lay, flexible, open, and non-liturgical approach that contemporary Pentecostals take to the sacrament of Holy Communion serves to underscore the sense of freedom and democratisation that comes with the experiences of the Spirit. Within experiential piety, structure and authority seems to have given way to liberty and freedom. What matters for contemporary Pentecostals in their celebration of the sacrament of Holy Communion is not so much the need to follow proper liturgical procedures, as the empowering benefits that are obtained from that sacrament because of the power of the Spirit working through the blood of Christ. This inclusive approach to communion and its virtual demystification through open access to all born again believers are strengths of a Christianity that has proven very attractive to Africa's upwardly mobile young people, who find the traditions of historic mission Christianity encumbering.

Bible-Believing and Bible Preaching Churches

The translation of the Bible into the vernacular contributed significantly to the spread and growth of Christianity in Africa. This is a fact attested by many leading African scholars and has been said to be the single most important legacy of Western missionary activity and, in some cases, the foundation of a new literacy culture which did not exist previously. This chapter reflects on the innovative uses to which the Bible is put in popular African Pentecostalism beyond its primary purpose as reading material for Christian edification. In most cases preaching and teaching were biblically relevant, even if not always theologically accurate.

The Bible in Christian Spirituality

The Bible is described by James Packer as the book in which 'the saving words of God are recorded and explained in a way that is wholly true, trustworthy, and therefore normative for faith'. In African Pentecostalism the Bible has acquired other uses apart from its purpose as a sacred book for Christian instruction. One of these is the declaration of biblical promises, especially using the words of the King James Version (KJV), which are considered more powerful than the simpler translated versions such as the Living Bible. The archaic English and weighty words of the KJV carry for users a certain supernatural import that the modern-English versions have lost in the process of translation. Contemporary Pentecostal preaching selectively picks up key words from the Bible, including phrases and sentences amounting to promises, and plays on them constantly by declaring them fulfilled either in 'the name of Jesus' or in the 'power of the Holy Spirit'.

Gordon Fee has observed that the Pentecostal attitude towards Scripture has often included a disregard for 'scientific exegesis' and carefully thought-out hermeneutics. For example, some of the choices that Jacob made in the Old Testament, no matter how morally wrong they were, are interpreted as 'smart moves' or 'skilful negotiations' needed to succeed in today's turbulent, capitalist, consumerist, and competitive world. In contemporary African Pentecostal understanding therefore, the end may sometimes justify the means.

Biblical Relativism

If Christianity is doing well in Africa, it is partly because African Christians do not compromise on the divinity and sacredness of the Bible. Elements of Western scholarship have downgraded the Bible and, in the process, Christianity has continued to lose its value as a faith with certain moral absolutes. Packer writes that some modern Westerners, whether outside or inside Christian communions, find it hard to believe that God can speak to human beings intelligibly in any sense at all and whenever the Bible is not allowed to have the last word on any matters of belief or behaviour, there the Bible is being relativized to human opinion.

In contradistinction to this liberal position found in many area of Western thought, African Christians, particularly those who belong to the independent indigenous charismatic streams, celebrate the divinity and supernatural status of the Bible. African Christian use of the Bible as a symbol of sacred power – as, for example, when it is placed under the pillow of a sleeping infant to provide protection from evil – does not in any way undermine its didactic use.

If the contents of the Bible are to be taken seriously as God's inspired word, the status of the Bible as a sacred book must first be recognised. The word of God in textual form is essentially material to be read and meditated upon, material that provides guidance through life and in relationships with God (Deut. 6:3). This is how Pentecostals read scripture.

Bible, Reformation, Renewal

Since the Reformation, the Bible has served as the fundamental source for the study of theology in the Christian world. Sound theology depends on sound interpretation of Scripture. The role of the Scriptures in the expansion of the Christian church in Africa is immeasurable. Reformations and renewals occur in the life of the church because God confronts his church afresh through his revealed Word, from which she may have drifted. The first fundamental Reformation tenet of *sola scriptura* stressed the preaching of the Word concentrated on showing that Scripture is necessary for humankind to know God.

In contemporary African Christianity, a majority of the young people who drift away from the historic mission denominations to join independently initiated Pentecostal/charismatic churches do so citing the lack of sound biblical teaching in the older churches. In response, charismatic renewal movements have emerged within the older churches and one of their main aims has been to turn the hearts of God's people to the Bible.

If Christianity is growing in Africa, it is partly because in African pulpits and homes, the Bible has found refuge as the authoritative Word of God. In one of the earliest independent churches in Ghana, a copy of the Bible is kept perpetually on the speakers' table, as a symbol of God's authority and presence among his people as they gather in worship. It also serves the church as a ritual symbol during healing sessions and symbolic or talismanic uses of the Bible are quite common in Africa, particularly in independent indigenous Christianity.

The inherent power of the Bible, as with all sacred substances, could be both helpful and dangerous. On one hand, by putting it under the pillow of a sleeping infant or tying it around the stomach of a pregnant woman, the Bible became for many a therapeutic means of restoring of health and providing protection. On the other hand, African Christians believe that if the Bible is not treated with the appropriate reverence and awe, it could also bring danger to its handlers.

African Christians have been made all too familiar with the fate of those who attempted to touch the Ark of the Covenant when they were not authorised to do so. The same principle whereby one places oneself in danger through inappropriate action is seen daily in the courts of law, where Christians are required to swear by the Bible to tell the truth. This use of the Bible is part of the colonial heritage. The practice continues the belief that if a person swears by the Bible and then tells a lie in a court of law, God, in whose name the oath was taken, will afflict the culprit with misfortune or even death.

Revelation, Inspiration and Authority

One of the things that has sustained the presence of Christianity in Africa is the evangelical approach to the Bible. It is expected of Christians that they will take the contents of the Scriptures seriously, and to do this, the Bible, as a sacred book, must be treated with a certain reverence and awe. If the Bible is the word of God, then in the African imagination, it must be endued with power. In the African traditional context, words, especially if spoken in the name of a supernatural being like a holy God, have performative effects. It is this mindset that has determined how the Bible and its contents have been appropriated in African Christianity.

In the Old Testament the written text as the Word of God serves symbolic purposes. For example, Moses told the Israelites: 'Tie them [the commandments] as symbols on your hands and bind them on your foreheads. Write them on the doorframes of your houses and on your gates.' (Deut. 6:8-9) Christian liturgical practices have shown the same reverence for the Bible by using it both as a written text for expository purposes and as a symbol of God's Word. In Reformed churches in Ghana, an open Bible is often kept on the altar during services as an affirmation of the Protestant principle that God's Word must be accessible to the people of God. A copy of the Bible is given to candidates for ordination and the instruction, 'Take thou authority to fulfil the office of a minister in the Church of Christ', is spoken. The presentation of the Bible is accompanied by words that seek to draw the attention of the candidates to its primary purpose: 'Brethren, give heed unto reading, exhortation, and doctrine. Think upon the things contained in the Holy Bible which we have now delivered unto you.'

In other words, the ability to take the contents of the Bible seriously is dependent on the weight that is placed on the Bible as the authoritative *holy* Word of God and its treatment as such. We find that popular African Christianity looks at sacramental and symbolic uses of the Bible, and these practices were not implemented at the neglect of reading of the text. There is no disconnect between, on one hand, the textual and hermeneutical uses of the Bible and, on the other, the talismanic uses to which African Christians put it. The contention of this chapter has been that their reverential attitude to the Bible has helped African Christians also take its contents seriously.

Conclusion: 'The Spirit Moveth'

Each of the themes discussed in the chapters of this book serves to illustrate how the movement of the Holy Spirit has changed the face of Christianity in Africa since the days of the establishment of historic mission denominations. Whether we are talking about lay participation in Christian ministry, or tithing and offerings, or new interpretations of Holy Communion, or the emphasis on anointing as a sacrament, we are dealing with interpretations of Christianity and forms of spirituality that take shape as people feel led by the Holy Spirit.

In human hands, anything can go wrong. Incorrect interpretations of Scripture and the inability of African prosperity evangelists to relate to the poor must not be taken to mean that the whole movement is an aberration. On this side of heaven, no Christianity is perfect, but the various pneumatic movements and churches allow us to glimpse what it means for the Spirit of God to be on the move. The mere fact that the movements whose spirituality has been under study here have come to the attention of the academy and have forced historic mission churches to undertake reforms is an indication that there is much that is positive about them and that we need to take them seriously. In particular, contemporary Pentecostalism has thrown up some incredibly gifted individuals, pastors, bishops, and general overseers of churches and ministries functioning in the power or anointing of the Spirit in the same way that the apostles did in the early years of the church, as recorded in the Acts of the Apostles.

Because of these pneumatic movements, the face of Christianity in Africa has changed perpetually. Some of the movements will survive, others will dwindle, but on the whole these ministries appear to me to be the future of Christianity on the continent. It does not mean that everything they are doing and preaching must be endorsed, but when people and ministries function in the power of the moving Spirit, there is transformation. In the experiential movements we have studied here, we see emerging new forms and interpretations of Christian spirituality that go beyond the limits of systematic theology as developed in the Western theology academy. African Pentecostal or pneumatic emphases on healing, worship, lay-participation in ministry, anointing, giving and tithing, and its interpretation of the Bible and application of the Bible to existential situations must all be brought on board in the study of theology.

In this attempt to interpret the nature, spirituality, and theology of pneumatic Christianity in Africa, I have relied on personal observations and experiences. In that process I have also criticised the excesses and misinterpretations that have resulted from uncritical approaches to Scripture and experience. It is expedient to conclude with consideration of a number of important theological and mission indicators that one needs to look for when the Spirit of God is genuinely on the move. I term these signs the 'benchmarks of

Pentecost' because in Africa, every single pneumatic movement has appealed to the biblical Pentecost for legitimacy. These are the criteria from which one could conclude, with some measure of certainty, that the Spirit of God, who worked in the apostles at Pentecost, is also at work in the church today. In other words, how does one judge that the Spirit of God is present or that an experience of Pentecost is giving rise to pneumatic movements in Christian mission? At least five benchmarks must be present, intertwined, to clearly signal that God is present in a place or working within a community by his Spirit.

1. Transformation into the Likeness of Jesus Christ

The most fundamental evidence that Pentecost has occurred in a person's life or within a community of faith is that lives have been transformed. We encounter this transformation in testimonies heard at Pentecostal gatherings and in people whom we know to have transitioned from sinful lives into active participation in church life. God's Spirit is qualified by the adjective 'holy'. That which is 'holy' is set apart from all profane and secular uses because it is filled with divine presence.

John Wesley spoke of this transformation when he said, 'my heart was strangely warmed'. He experienced the transforming presence of the Holy Spirit, which helped him to preach and pursue his theological agenda of Scriptural holiness even more forcefully. A church that is filled with the Spirit therefore also preaches very strongly against sin and moral depravity, because the more we experience the presence of the Spirit, the more we love to stay away from sin. African pneumatic movements have always challenged the moral laxity associated with historic mission Christianity, especially at the point when new churches are emerging.

2. Desire for Prayer and Renewal

When Pentecost occurred, the new community of believers studied the Word and prayed. A key manifestation of the Spirit is the ability to pray in tongues. There are several uses of tongues, but its primary function is private prayer. When we pray in tongues, Paul says, 'we speak mysteries unto God'. In Romans 8:26 Paul talks about the Spirit interceding for us with 'groans too deep for words'. When the Spirit of God is present, he inspires in us the spirit of prayer and this is usually accompanied by a new and intense desire to read the Word of God. An important contribution of pneumatic movements in Africa to the life of the church is found in their drawing of attention to charismatic renewal phenomena, especially tongues, as valid Christian experiences in worship.

3. Empowerment for Active Witness

The expression 'empowerment' is important to understanding the place of the Spirit in the lives of renewal movements. Paul makes reference to having been given the 'strength' to do all things in Philippians 4:13. We see also that Jesus Christ 'breathed' on the disciples at the point of commissioning them after the resurrection, meaning that he empowered them to witness. The presence of the Holy Spirit made their witness effective, as Paul attests also. Indeed in Colossians 1:28, Paul talks about proclaiming Christ and 'admonishing and teaching everyone with all wisdom'.

Energy and power go together, so the energy that was at work in Paul and enabled him to perform his ministry was none other than the power of the Holy Spirit. The Holy Spirit activates the Presence of God in the believer and in the church, enabling them to engage in active witness, because the granting of the Spirit and the sending of the disciples occurred in tandem. For this reason I explain the ministries of contemporary Pentecostals in terms of the Spirit of God being on the move.

4. *Manifestations of the Spirit*

It is unfortunate that the historic mission churches cringe when we talk about the gifts of the Spirit. Until they started tolerating renewal movements, these churches had ceded that part of their ministry to the Pentecostals and a few members of charismatic persuasion. The Christian community that the Spirit of God builds is always a charismatic community in which the graces of the Spirit, such as speaking in tongues, healing, prophecy, visions, and revelations, are present. How churches manage to abandon that tradition and opt for one in which the Spirit is virtually excluded from worship and ministry remains a mystery. The church of the New Testament was charismatic and the rise of pneumatic movements in Africa throws out an urgent challenge to the rest of the church to be open to the presence of the Spirit, manifest not just in its ministry, but also among people of faith. The gifts and manifestations of the Spirit are not denomination specific. They are for the body of Christ and all Christians belong to that body.

5. Pursuit of Eternal Values

When Pentecost came, those who experienced the presence of the Spirit turned their back on the world. They pursued those things that were indicators of Kingdom values, the greatest of which, Paul says, is the virtue of love. Love was reflected in their fellowship; it showed in the way the members cared for each other; and it was evident in the lifestyle they adopted. Our ultimate example of love is Jesus himself, who did not count equality with God as something to be grasped but emptied himself for the world out of love. The Spirit of God births love in the hearts of God's people and where he displays his presence, love is always present. If understood thus, the collection of tithes and the holding of anointing services, for example, will be devoid of exploitation and showmanship and done to the glory of God.

African pneumatic movements testify to the fact that Pentecost is both a historical and present reality. It is a historical reality because it happened as Jesus Christ promised. It is a present reality because we all need to experience our Pentecost as individuals and as a church. Without Pentecost, it is just impossible to function the way God expects us to function as Christians. Similarly, a church that does not have the Spirit of God is never effective as a witnessing community. It may have a form of religion, but usually lacks the power of it! It is the power of the Spirit that has led the presence of Christianity to shift from the global North to the global South, as is testified by contemporary Pentecostalism, the representative face of Christianity in Africa.